A First Book of
COWBOY SONGS

A First Book of
COWBOY SONGS

21 Favorite Songs in Easy Piano Arrangements

with Downloadable MP3s

Dolly M. Moon
Assistant Director, The Music School, Brooklyn, N.Y.

Illustrated by
MARTY NOBLE

DOVER PUBLICATIONS, INC.
Mineola, New York

All songs available as downloadable MP3s!

Go to: http://www.doverpublications.com/0486243117
to access these files.

*This book is dedicated to the memory of Sasha
Backer, who was a student at The Music School
1977-78.*

Bibliographical Note

A First Book of Cowboy Songs is a retitled republication of *My
Very First Book of Cowboy Songs: 21 Favorite Songs in Easy Piano
Arrangements,* first published by Dover Publications, Inc., in 1982.
Original illustrations by Marty Noble were added to the 1999
reprint of this title.

International Standard Book Number

ISBN-13: 978-0-486-24311-5
ISBN-10: 0-486-24311-7

Manufactured in the United States by LSC Communications
24311717   2017
www.doverpublications.com

Contents

	page
Goodbye, Ol' Paint	1
Ev'ry Night When the Sun Goes In	2
I'm Going to Leave Old Texas	3
Red River Valley	4
My Darling Clementine (four hands)	6
Down in the Valley	9
She'll Be Coming 'Round the Mountain	10
Sweet Betsy from Pike	12
The Cowboy	14
Strawberry Roan	15
The Boll Weevil	18
On Top of Old Smoky	20
My Home's in Montana	21
Nelly Bly (four hands)	22
The Lone Prairie	25
Shenandoah	26
Home on the Range	28
Here, Rattler, Here (four hands)	30
The Rainbow Cradle	33
Nebraska Boys	34
The Streets of Laredo	36

Goodbye, Ol' Paint

Cowboy Song

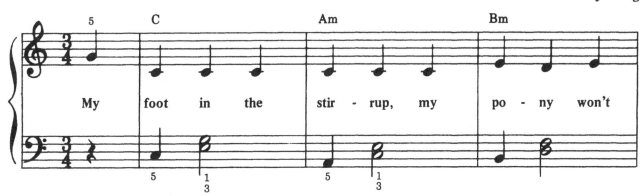

My foot in the stir - rup, my po - ny won't

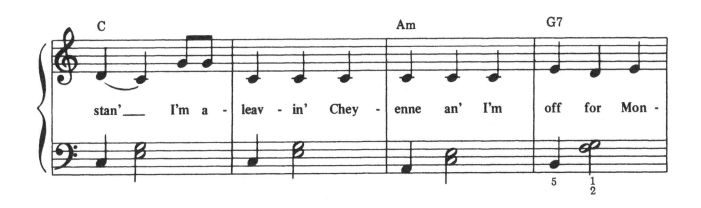

stan'___ I'm a - leav - in' Chey - enne an' I'm off for Mon -

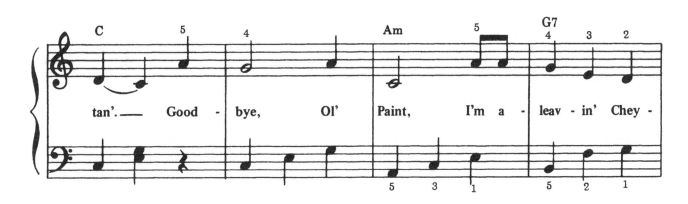

tan'.___ Good - bye, Ol' Paint, I'm a - leav - in' Chey -

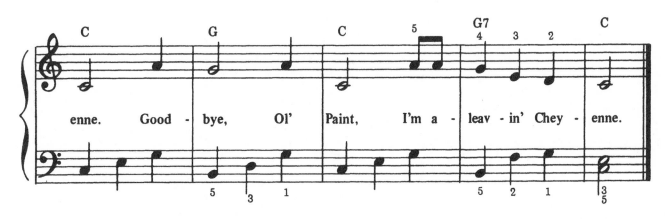

enne. Good - bye, Ol' Paint, I'm a - leav - in' Chey - enne.

1

Ev'ry Night When the Sun Goes In

American

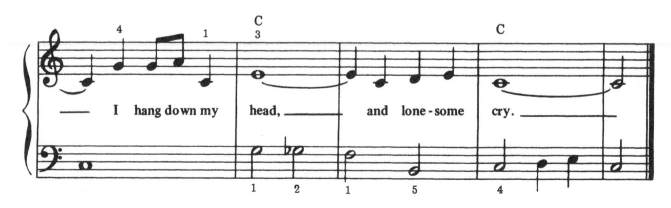

I'm Going to Leave Old Texas

I'm going to leave   old Tex - as   now.

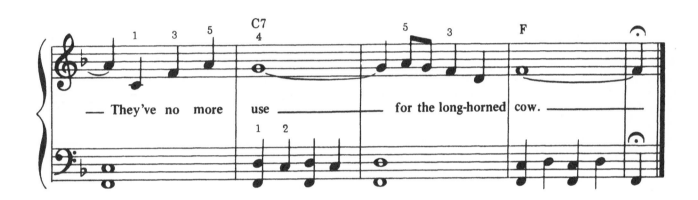

They've no more   use   for the long-horned cow.

2. They've plowed and fenced my cattle range,
And the people there are all so strange.

Red River Valley

American Song

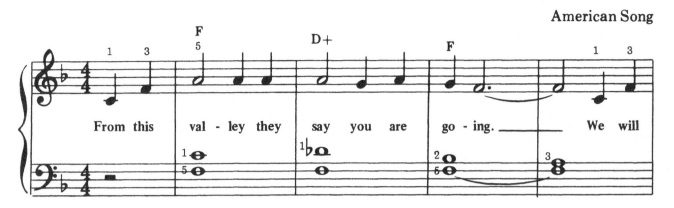

From this val - ley they say you are go - ing. _____ We will

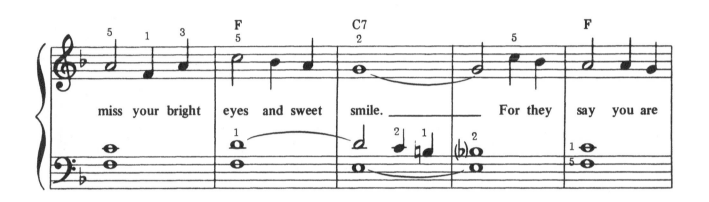

miss your bright eyes and sweet smile. _____ For they say you are

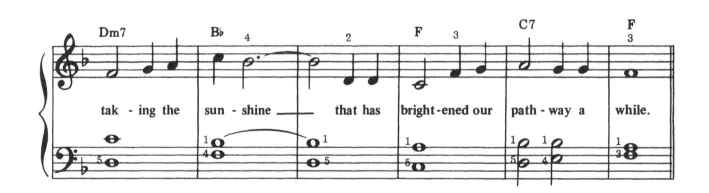

tak - ing the sun - shine _____ that has bright-ened our path - way a while.

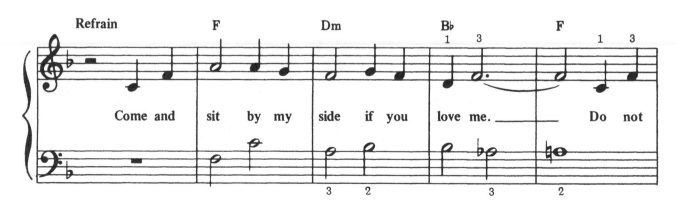

Come and sit by my side if you love me. _____ Do not

has - ten to bid me a - dieu. _____ Just re - mem - ber the Red Riv - er

Val - ley, _____ and the one who has loved you so true. _____

My Darling Clementine

(secondo)

Traditional

My Darling Clementine

(primo)

Traditional

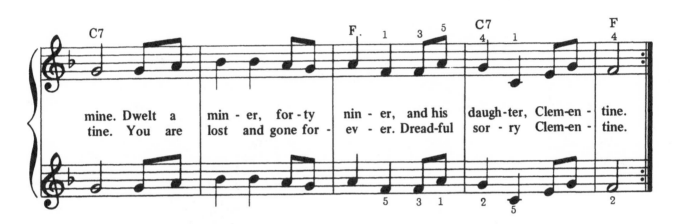

Verse 1. In a cav - ern, in a can - yon, ex - ca - vat - ing for a mine. Dwelt a min - er, for - ty nin - er, and his daugh - ter, Clem-en - tine.

Chorus: Oh, my dar - ling, oh, my dar - ling, oh, my dar - ling Clem-en - tine. You are lost and gone for - ev - er. Dread-ful sor - ry Clem-en - tine.

2. Light she was, and like a fairy,
And her shoes were number nine;
Herring boxes without topses
Sandals were for Clementine.

3. Drove she ducklings to the water
Ev'ry morning just at nine;
Hit her foot against a splinter,
Fell into the foaming brine.

4. Ruby lips above the water,
Blowing bubbles soft and fine;
But, alas, I was no swimmer,
So I lost my Clementine.

5. Then the miner, forty-niner,
Soon began to peak and pine;
Thought he oughter join his daughter.
Now he's with his Clementine.

6. In my dreams she still does haunt me,
Robed in garments soaked in brine;
Though in life I used to hug her,
Now she's dead, I draw the line.

7

Down in the Valley

Kentucky Mountain Song

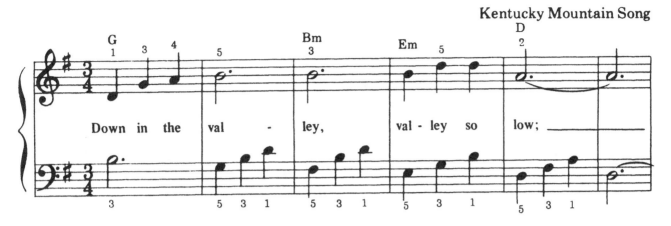

Down in the val - ley, val - ley so low; _____

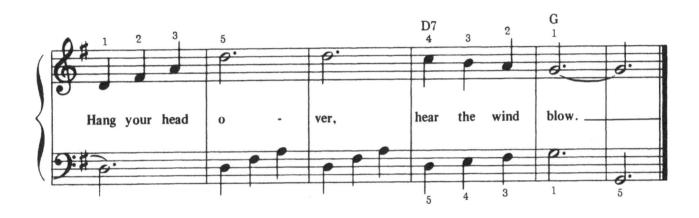

Hang your head o - ver, hear the wind blow. _____

2. Hear the wind blow, dear, hear the wind blow;
   Hang your head over, hear the wind blow.

She'll Be Coming 'Round the Mountain

American Folk Song

2. She'll be driving six white horses when she comes.

3. We will all go out to meet her when she comes.

4. We will kill the old red rooster when she comes.

5. We will have chicken and dumplings when she comes.

6. She'll be wearing wool pajamas when she comes.

7. She will have to sleep with Grandma when she comes.

Sweet Betsy from Pike

Traditional American

Oh, do you re - mem-ber sweet Bet - sy from Pike, who crossed the wide

prai - ries with her hus - band Ike? With two yoke of ox - en and

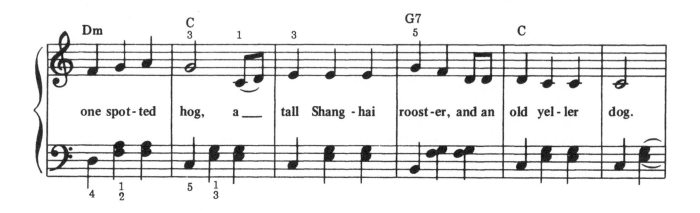

one spot - ted hog, a ___ tall Shang - hai roost-er, and an old yel - ler dog.

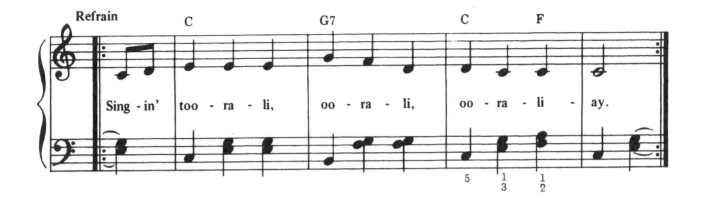

Refrain

Sing - in' too - ra - li,   oo - ra - li,   oo - ra - li - ay.

2. The Shanghai ran off and the cattle all died,
   The last piece of bacon that morning was fried;
   Poor Ike got discouraged, and Betsy got mad,
   The dog wagged his tail and looked wonderfully sad.

3. One morning they climbed up a very high hill,
   And with wonder looked down into old Placerville;
   Ike shouted and said, as he cast his eyes down,
   "Sweet Betsy, my darling, we've got to Hangtown."

The Cowboy

Old Texas Melody
Words by MAYME CHRISTENSON

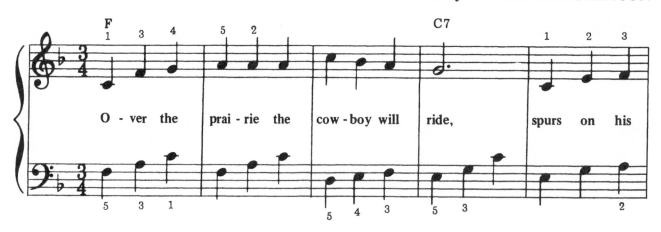

O - ver the prai - rie the cow - boy will ride, spurs on his

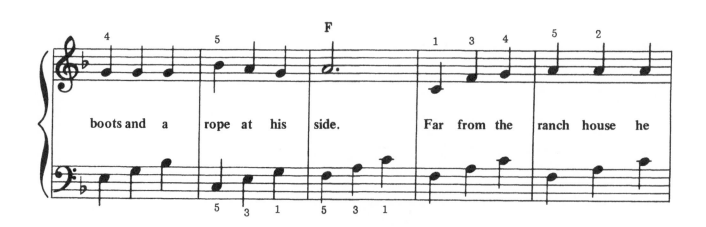

boots and a rope at his side. Far from the ranch house he

trav - els each day, yip - pee - ki, yip - pee - ki, yip - pee - ki - yay!

Strawberry Roan

Cowboy Song

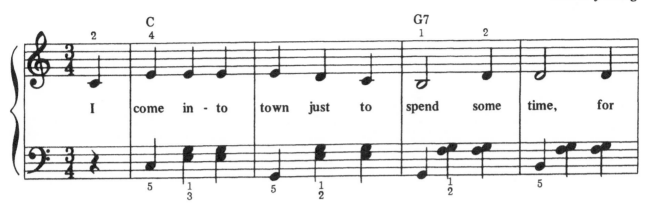

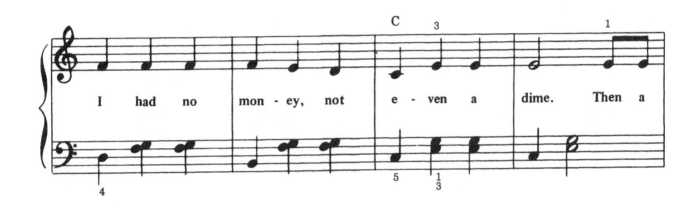

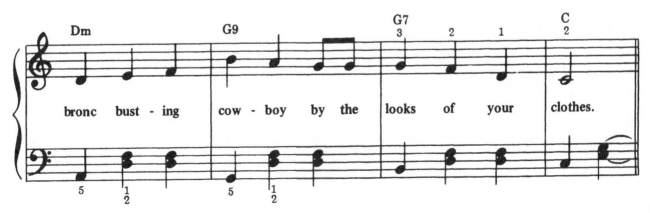

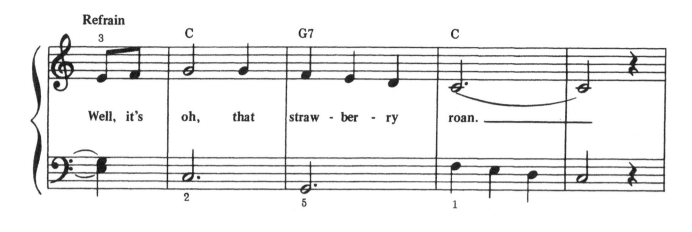

Refrain

C   G7   C

Well, it's   oh,   that   straw - ber - ry   roan. _____

F   C   F

Oh,   that   straw - ber - ry   roan. _____ That   straw - ber - ry

C   Dm

po - ny no   one ev - er   rode,   and the   cow - boy that   tries it is

C   G7   C

sure to get   thrown!   Oh,   that   straw - ber - ry   roan! _____

2. "You've guessed me just right! I'm your man," I
   claim.
   "Do you have a wild horse you'd like me to tame?"
   Well, he said that he had, and a bad one to buck,
   And for throwing good riders, the horse had good
   luck.

3. I jumped on his back and I held the reins;
   That strawberry horse threw me off for my pains.
   So I climbed on again to the horse's surprise,
   And he tried then to throw me right up to the skies.

The Boll Weevil

Texas Folk Song

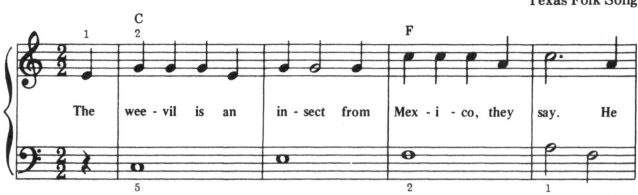

The wee-vil is an in-sect from Mex-i-co, they say. He

trav-eled up to Tex-as, and he thought he'd bet-ter stay. Just a-look-in' for a

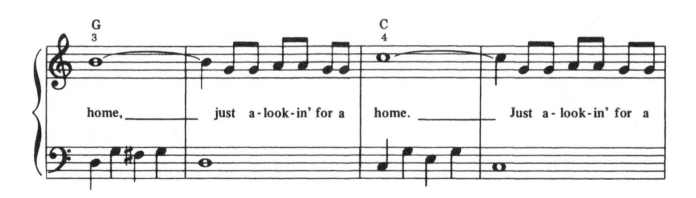

home, _____ just a-look-in' for a home. _____ Just a-look-in' for a

home, _____ just a-look-in' for a home.

2. First time I saw the weevil, he's sittin' on the square.
   The next time that I saw him, he had all his family there.
   Just a-lookin' for a home (etc.).

3. Last time I saw the weevil, he'd settled down for life;
   He'd brought his aunts and uncles, his cousin and his wife.
   They're a-lookin' for a home (etc.).

On Top of Old Smoky

Kentucky Mountain Song

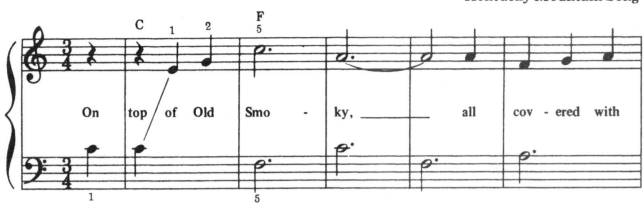

On top of Old Smo - ky, ____ all cov - ered with

snow. ____ I lost my true lov - er ____

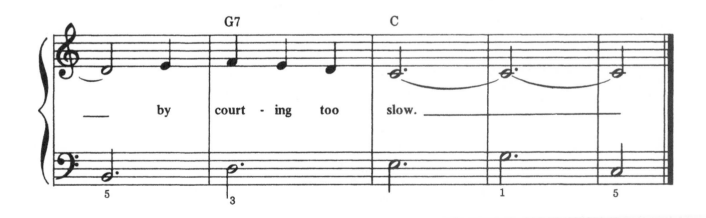

___ by court - ing too slow. ____

2. A-courting is pleasure, and parting is grief,
But a false-hearted lover is worse than a thief.

My Home's in Montana

Cowboy Song

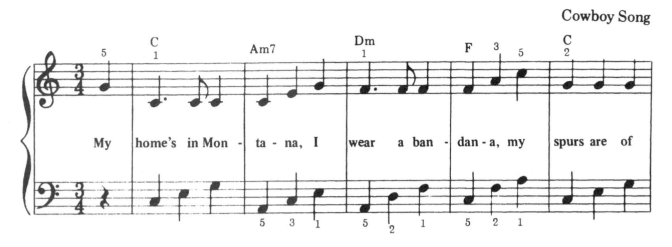

My home's in Mon - ta - na, I wear a ban - dan - a, my spurs are of

sil - ver, my po - ny is gray. When rid - ing the rang - es, my

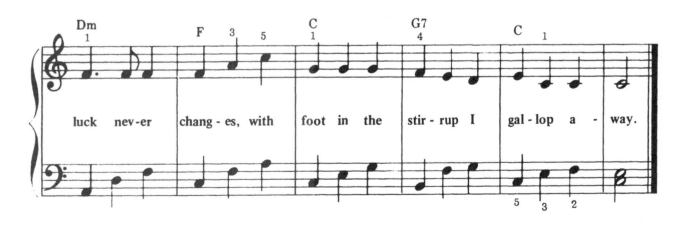

luck nev - er chang - es, with foot in the stir - rup I gal - lop a - way.

Nelly Bly

(secondo)

STEPHEN FOSTER

Chorus

Nelly Bly

(primo)

STEPHEN FOSTER

Nel - ly Bly, Nel - ly Bly, bring the broom a - long; we'll
Poke the wood, la - dy love, make the fire burn; and

sweep the kitch - en clean my dear, and have a lit - tle song.
while I take my ban - jo down, just give the mush a turn.

Chorus

Heigh! Nel - ly, ho! Nel - ly, lis - ten, love, to me! I'll

sing for you, play for you a dul - cet mel - o - dy.

2. Nelly Bly has a voice like the turtle dove;
   I hear it in the meadow, and I hear it in the grove.
   Nelly Bly has a heart warm as a cup of tea,
   And bigger than the sweet potato down in Tennes-
   see.

3. Nelly Bly shuts her eyes when she goes to sleep,
   And when she wakens up again her eyeballs 'gin to
   peep.
   The way she walks, she lifts her foot, and then she
   puts it down,

And when it falls there's music there in that part
of the town.

4. Nelly Bly, Nelly Bly! Never, never sigh.
   Never bring the teardrop to the corner of your eye.
   For the pie is made of pumpkins, and the mush is
   made of corn,
   And there's corn and pumpkins plenty, love, a-
   lyin' in the barn.

The Lone Prairie

Traditional

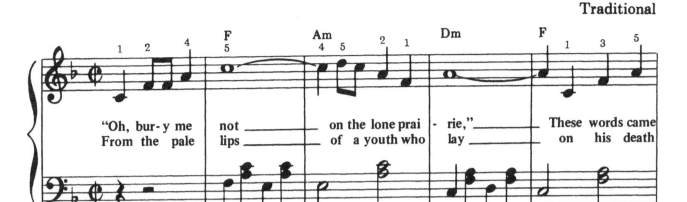

"Oh, bur-y me not _____ on the lone prai - rie," _____ These words came
From the pale lips _____ of a youth who lay _____ on his death

low _____ and mourn-ful - ly. _____
bed _____ at the close of day. _____

2. "Oh, bury me not on the lone prairie
Where the coyotes howl and the wind blows free.
In a cold, cold grave don't bury me,
Oh, bury me not on the lone prairie."

3. "Oh, bury me not—" and his voice failed there.
But we took no heed of his dying prayer;
In a narrow grave just six by three
We buried him there on the lone prairie.

Shenandoah

Traditional

Oh, Shen-an-doah, I long to hear you, way,— hey, you roll-ing

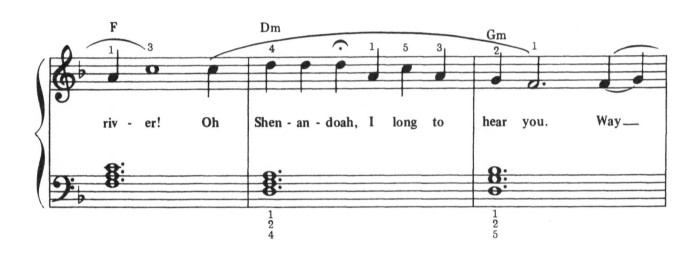

riv - er! Oh Shen - an - doah, I long to hear you. Way—

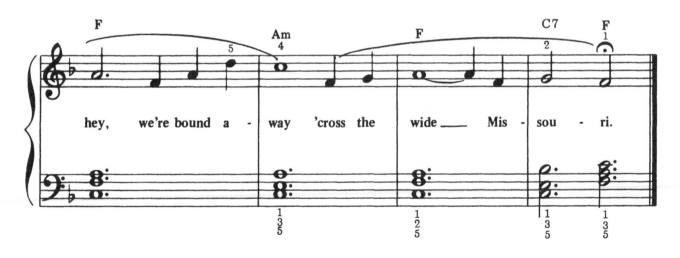

hey, we're bound a - way 'cross the wide —— Mis - sou - ri.

2. Oh, Shenandoah, I love your daughter.
Way, hey, you rolling river!
Oh, Shenandoah, I love your daughter.
Way, hey, we're bound away
'Cross the wide Missouri.

3. Oh, Shenandoah, I'm bound to leave you.
Way, hey, you rolling river!
Oh, Shenandoah, I'll not deceive you.
Way, hey, we're bound away
'Cross the wide Missouri.

Home on the Range

Cowboy Song

O, give me a home, where the buf - fa - lo

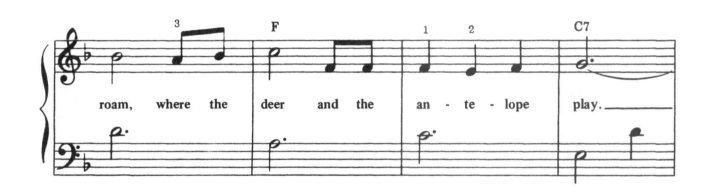

roam, where the deer and the an - te - lope play.____

____ Where sel - dom is heard a dis - cour - ag - ing

word, and the skies are not cloud - y all day.____

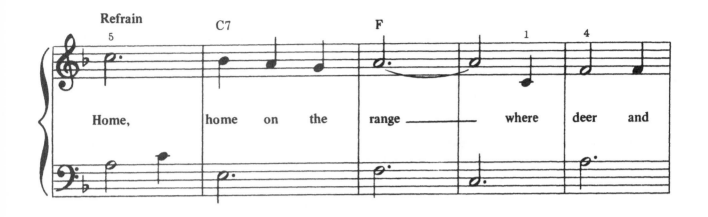

Home, home on the range _____ where deer and

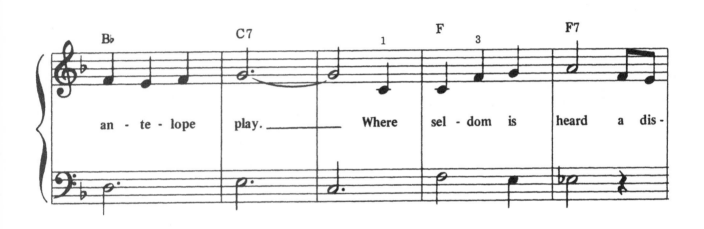

an - te - lope play. _____ Where sel - dom is heard a dis-

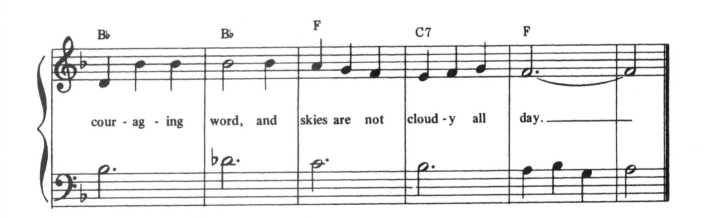

cour - ag - ing word, and skies are not cloud - y all day. _____

Here, Rattler, Here

(secondo)

American Folk Song

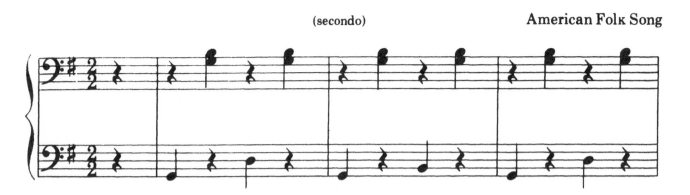

Refrain

G

D

Here,   Rat - tler,   here!   Here,   Rat - tler,   here.

D7

G

Call   Rat - tler   from   the   barn,   Here,   Rat - tler,   here!

8va ♩

Here, Rattler, Here

(primo)

American Folk Song

2. Oh, once I had a setting hen, set her as you know;
   Set her on six dozen eggs and hatched out one old crow.

3. Old Rattler's dead and gone, alas, gone where good dogs go.
   Better watch out and don't play dog, or you'll be a goner, too.

The Rainbow Cradle

Navajo Indian Song

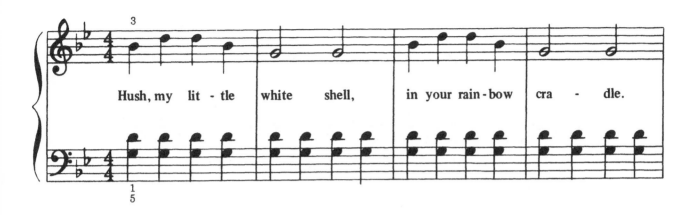

Hush, my lit-tle white shell, in your rain-bow cra - dle.

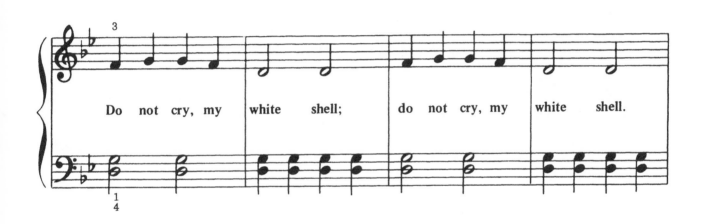

Do not cry, my white shell; do not cry, my white shell.

Go to sleep, my white shell; go to sleep, my white shell.

2. Rainbows lie beneath you, downy clouds around you.
Hush, my little white shell; do not cry, my white shell.
Go to sleep, my white shell; go to sleep, my white shell.

Nebraska Boys

American Folk Song

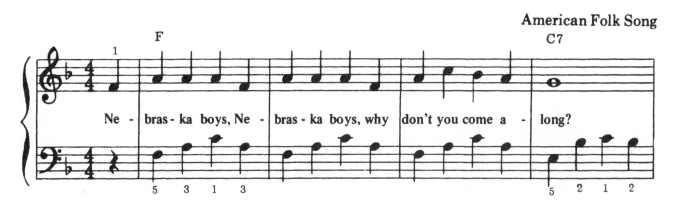

Ne - bras - ka boys, Ne - bras - ka boys, why don't you come a - long?

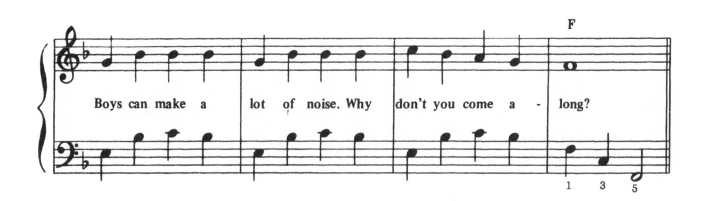

Boys can make a lot of noise. Why don't you come a - long?

Refrain

Hey, hey, hey, hey, why don't you come a - long?

Hey, hey, hey, hey, why don't you come a - long?

2. Nebraska girls, Nebraska girls, why don't you come along?
   Sky-blue eyes and pretty curls. Why don't you come along?

The Streets of Laredo

Traditional

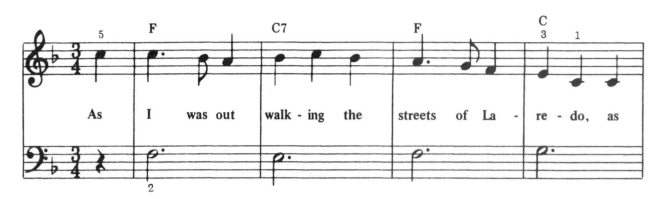

As I was out walk - ing the streets of La - re - do, as

I walked out in La - re - do one day, I met a young cow-boy all

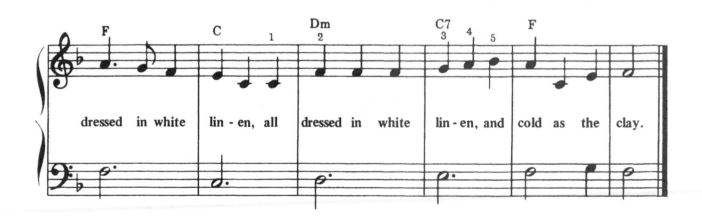

dressed in white lin - en, all dressed in white lin - en, and cold as the clay.

2. "I see by your outfit that you are a cowboy,"
   These words he did say as I boldly stepped by.
   "Come sit down beside me and hear my sad story;
   I was shot in the breast and I know I must die."

3. "O beat the drum slowly and play the fife lowly,
   And play the dead march as you bear me along.
   Take me to the green valley and lay the sod o'er me,
   For I'm a young cowboy and I know I've done wrong."